Deeply Rooted

Mindful practices for cultivating self-compassion, self-acceptance & healing

a guided journal

PEGGY OLIVEIRA, MSW

Published by: Courageous Journeys®
Email: healing@courageousjourneys.com

Ordering Information:

Quantity sales. Special discounts may be available on quantity purchases by non-profits, associations, and others. Email inquiry to address above with Subject: Quantity Sales.

Deeply Rooted - Peggy Oliveira - First Edition

ISBN 978-1-7360508-7-3

ISBN 978-1-7360508-1-1

Deeply Rooted is a mindful, guided journal with prompts, practices, and exercises to help you connect with self-compassion and release self-judgment and shame so you may be *deeply rooted* in self-acceptance.

When we are able to wholly accept ourselves, with all our humanly imperfections, we experience a grounded sense of confidence and emotional freedom.

This journal guides you through a process with practices you can return to as you navigate your journey of becoming healthy, happy, whole, and free.

With deepest gratitude

For all those I've had the honor of guiding on their courageous journey of emotional healing. Your courage and vulnerability will forever continue to inspire me. And to you, the reader, who chose me to accompany you on your journey of cultivating self-compassion and coming home to you.

To my husband, thank you for believing in me when I was not able to believe in myself and always providing unlimited support to me and all my endeavors.

There could be several reasons you may have chosen this book. A desire to feel more peace within; build confidence; release self-doubt; forgive yourself (for real or perceived mistakes or flaws); release guilt; or heal shame.

Whatever led you to pick up this book, I'm so glad you did! It means you know the freedom you've been desiring is available to you.

Self-compassion is the path to wholehearted self-acceptance.

Why is self-compassion important?

We live in a world with systems that perpetuate the idea we must continue to do more or be better, smarter, fitter, kinder, prettier, wealthier, more successful... the list is never-ending.

It is virtually impossible to not have at least some moments when we struggle with self-doubt. For many of us, the moments are too many to count.

It may be in our roles as a parent, friend, daughter or son, employee, boss, or leader.

It may be in how we show up in the world... how we behave and what we do or don't do.

It may be about mistakes made, even very unintentional ones.

It may even be in things we have no control over like how we look or how our body functions or struggles to function.

These ongoing moments lead to or reinforce beliefs about who we are... often, on some level, about not being *enough*.

And, our beliefs dictate how we think, feel, and show up in the world.

Take a moment to notice any thoughts, ideas, reflections, feelings, or body sensations present.

Self-compassion is the antidote to any judgment, doubt, or criticism you've been holding onto about yourself.

It is not possible to hold judgment while you mindfully experience self-compassion.

As you build your capacity for self-compassion, you naturally shift how you experience moments of self-doubt and mistakes.

Instead of going to the depths of all the negative things you believe about yourself or feel the pain of shame, your more natural response becomes one of compassion, kindness, and acceptance.

A lack of self-compassion is at the core of our personal struggle with being able to feel happy, whole and free... within ourselves, our relationships, and with the world around us.

If we are not mindful about practicing self-compassion we naturally "practice" self-judgment, guilt, or shame.

So, why does self-compassion matter? So we may live our lives deeply rooted in self-acceptance. When we are able to wholly accept ourselves as we are there is a grounded knowing in this simple truth...we are ***always,*** in ***all ways*** enough.

Only when we experience self-compassion can we be deeply connected within. Only when we are deeply connected within can we be deeply connected to others.

What is self-compassion?

Self-compassion is simply a mindful moment of kindness, understanding, or acceptance of yourself as you are in any given moment.

It's the ability to honor your humanness in the moments when you make a mistake.

It's forgiving yourself when your actions have let yourself or someone else down.

Self-compassion is acknowledging personal limitations without those limitations defining who you believe you are.

It's a recognition that your expectations of yourself may be beyond what is possible for any one individual or for yourself in *that* moment. *Hello perfectionist, I'm speaking to you!*

Self-compassion is a *practice*. The more we practice, the more natural it becomes and the more impact it has.

What self-compassion is not...

An abdication of personal responsibility. Self-indulgent. Self-pitying.

Becoming an emotionally healthy and whole human requires us to be able to hold both, our imperfection and responsibility (perceived or real) in times when our actions or words may lead to undesirable or unintentional consequences for ourselves or others.

Self-compassion is the path to this wholeness.

Some examples of self-compassionate statements or affirmations:

It's okay that ________ .

I am perfectly imperfect!

I can forgive myself for this as I would so easily forgive someone else.

Struggling with ________ does not make me bad or weak. It makes me human.

We all have strengths or areas we excel in and areas that are challenging. Our challenges do not make us less valuable.

My mistakes do not define my worthiness.

I am as deserving of my compassion and kindness as those I love.

Why I believe in the healing power of self-compassion.

Over the past 20 years in my work as a therapist, I have witnessed the depth and breadth of the impact of self-judgment, guilt, self-criticism, and shame, in varying degrees, on nearly every client I've worked with.

It can range from a nagging experience of never feeling truly whole, no matter what you achieve or how much inner work you've done, to having relentless and often debilitating thoughts and feelings that can create difficulty in relationships and contribute to symptoms of depression and anxiety.

All this impacts how we move through our days, the choices we make for our lives, the partners and friends we choose... or don't, and what we allow ourselves to imagine possible for our lives.

Through my own struggle and healing process as a childhood trauma survivor, I gained a deep understanding of the felt experience of these emotions and the subsequent self-acceptance and freedom that comes from the practice of self-compassion.

This practice has also been incredibly valuable in my role as a parent to lessen anxiety of my imperfection and worry about creating lasting damage to the psyche of my children (ugh, parental guilt is real!).

Before I began my healing journey, and even through its early stages, I perceived most things I did as somehow wrong, bad, or not good enough. So, with each action (or non-action, I was a huge procrastinator) there was at least a moment of judgment. Depending on what the situation was, there were often days filled with judgment which could easily lead to shame and a desire to isolate, creating more disconnection and struggle.

Much of the work I do with clients is helping them ground into a deep understanding and practice of self-compassion.

While self-compassion is simple in theory, it is anything but in practice.

I am often met with eye rolls, rebuttals, and sometimes even anxious resistance when I talk about self-compassion because it can seem antithesis to everything they've known and experienced.

Most people are great at feeling and showing others compassion but the idea of turning that kindness and care inward can feel uncertain and possibly unattainable.

While it may not be simple or easy, shifting from self-judgment to self-compassion is possible with intentional effort and practice.

The exercises in this journal are designed for you to come back to as a practice and reminder as you continue on your journey.

You deserve to be free of any judgment, doubt, and/or shame you've been holding onto. You deserve to have the emotional freedom that comes naturally when you are deeply rooted in self-acceptance.

Exploring, using, and integrating this journal and practices.

Cultivating self-compassion is a *process* and a *practice.*

We must consciously work to notice when we're not being nice to ourselves then work to change the automatic response (thoughts/feelings/behaviors) by identifying and connecting with a different message...

A message based in truth, understanding, acceptance... **compassion**.

This is not typically easy for most of us. It can feel frustrating, aggravating, overwhelming, and impossible at times.

These feelings can then reinforce the not-so-nice (false) beliefs we hold about ourselves.

Most people have negative thoughts go through their mind many times a day. Some days, several hundred times.

Sometimes they're conscious (you notice the thought) and sometimes they're subconscious (you don't notice you're saying anything to yourself at all).

We often hold on to mistakes we've made and hurtful experiences as "proof" of the negative beliefs we have about who we are.

They become the reasons we believe we're undeserving, not enough, not capable, etc.

When you get or do something "wrong" it becomes a piece of "evidence" we continue to point to and hold on to in order to reinforce these beliefs.

In the context of this journal, I use the term mistake to identify things you may feel badly about. It could be a genuine mistake that was completely unintentional. It may be a choice you've made that had negative consequences for yourself or someone else. Or, something that has left you feeling badly about who you are, leading to feelings of guilt or shame.

Learning to acknowledge and take responsibility (when appropriate) for mistakes or regrettable choices and not going to a place of shame is an important part of healing and overall mental well-being.

Sometimes self-forgiveness is necessary, **ALWAYS** self-compassion is necessary.

This guided journal contains exercises to help you gain understanding, practice, and integrate a deeply rooted sense of self-acceptance through self-compassion.

As you begin this journey, I'd like to encourage you to give yourself the time and space (both emotional and physical) to *be with* the practices.

Carve out a space and give yourself the time to work through the exercises. Consider choosing a space that feels welcoming, comfortable, and quiet. Maybe even light a candle or have a cup of tea.

The exercises and journal prompts are designed to help you navigate *through* obstacles that have kept you from being able to fully accept and honor who you are in **ALL** moments.

As a result, they may bring up thoughts, feelings, or reactions which may surprise you. You may feel some emotion come to the surface or you may feel some resistance. Resistance can feel similar to annoyance or look like distraction.

This is normal and can be a powerful moment of awareness. It can also be a beautiful opportunity to begin your practice of self-compassion, reminding yourself it's okay to feel what you feel.

Use the journaling space to write what comes up. Taking the time to notice and "be with" what is stirred helps you connect with what needs healing. These practices are an important tool to help you on that journey.

As you sit with the exercises in reflection and curiosity, not judgment or criticism, you'll deepen your connection within.... allowing you to deeply ground into embodied, whole self-acceptance and emotional freedom.

There are no right or wrong answers to any of the questions or prompts. What comes to mind one day may be quite different another day. The practices are designed to help you connect with where you are in a given moment. In one moment, any judgment may look or sound different than it would have a few days ago or a few days from now. And each judgment, when touched with self-compassion, allows for a release of its energy.

You can go through the journal in order or let your intuition guide you and randomly open to a practice. Either way, this journal is meant for you to come back to time and time again. Remember, it's a *practice.*

Anytime you're feeling a bit stressed or disconnected, this can help you reconnect and ground into what is real and true... nourishing your roots.

If you're struggling with some level of self-doubt or fear, the exercises can help you navigate the struggle and remind you of your inherent worthiness and capability.

Let's begin!

***Important self-care message.**

It is completely normal to have challenging thoughts and feelings come to the surface as you navigate a process of connecting within and emotional healing. It's important to honor and take care of yourself as they do or if things begin to feel more difficult than expected.

If you've not addressed emotional wounding, particularly childhood wounding, this may be the first time you connect a bit more deeply, witnessing your wounded heart.

Be gentle with yourself and remember, SELF-COMPASSION is the most loving witness to any unhealed pain.

If you notice an overall increase in anxious or depressive thoughts or find yourself struggling more emotionally, please reach out for support from a trusted professional. If you are a trauma survivor, I encourage a clinician who specializes in trauma healing.

I am as deserving of
my compassion,
understanding, and
kindness as those I love.

Take a few moments to reflect on what made you choose this journal.

Was it something you felt on an intuitive level?

Were you specifically looking for a resource to build self-compassion? Or maybe searching for something to help you feel *better* in some way?

What do you hope to experience as you work through this journal?

Take a moment to check in with what is present in your body. What does the air feel like on your skin? Do you notice any tension or constriction in your muscles or organs (notice your heart and lungs)?

When complete,

Inhale... Possibility

Exhale... Uncertainty

How has a lack of self-compassion impacted you... how you feel about who you are and how you show up in the world?

Take a moment to imagine what would be different if you were able to show yourself the same grace, understanding, kindness, and forgiveness you give to others.

If it feels comfortable to you, close your eyes and take a deep breath, visualize that difference. Connect to the feeling(s) in your body as you experience this compassion and acceptance.

Give yourself a few rounds of breath to sit with this.

Journal thoughts, reflections, and feelings brought up through this exercise.

There is no right or wrong way to think or feel about this. It's a practice to help you connect within.

Let yourself be proud of doing the courageous work of self-reflection and healing.

When complete,

Inhale... Courage

Exhale... Self-Doubt

If you don't mess things up at times, you're not fully living.

What self-compassionate words can you say to yourself when you feel like you've messed up or made a mistake?

This can be a struggle for many people. We tend to believe if we've done something wrong or bad, we are not deserving of kindness or understanding. Especially if our actions may have hurt someone else, even unintentionally.

The truth is, when we can be self-compassionate, it is much easier for us to take responsibility when we need to, to apologize in a deep and genuine way, and fully acknowledge our personal challenges without feeling ashamed of them.

All of this leads to emotional freedom that comes from rooted self-acceptance.

Here are some considerations for how you might give yourself more grace, kindness, forgiveness, and deeper understanding:

First, imagine what you would say to someone you care about. In most cases, if that person did, thought, or felt what you have, you'd likely be supportive of them. Even if they did something you didn't like, you'd still be able to see them as worthy of being cared for or forgiven. You might even view it as something not nearly as bad as they believe it is.

This is true for you as well!
Practice turning those same words towards yourself.

You can remind yourself you don't immediately turn your back on someone if they don't return your message right away, forget something you've shared with them, or cancel plans if they aren't feeling well.

If you can be accepting of them in these moments, doesn't it make sense you (and they) can be accepting of you in similar circumstances?

You can remind yourself that perfection doesn't exist. That we all make mistakes.

I'm sure there are many people you value, respect, enjoy, and love who've made mistakes. So, isn't it possible you can also be valued, respected, enjoyed, and loved exactly as you are, even when you make a mistake?

Notice any thoughts or body sensations.

Are you finding all the reasons why all this may be true for others but not for you?

Take a moment to sit with these ideas then write what feels present for you. What do you notice in your body? Do you feel some resonance with this, or do you find yourself wanting to resist?

When complete,

Inhale... Connection

Exhale... Isolation

Most of us find it quite natural to experience a sense of compassion for those around us, even for strangers.

However, when we think about ourselves... our struggles or mistakes, the energy of our thoughts often shifts to criticism or judgment.

We hear a disappointed, angry or critical voice in our head (sometimes our own, sometimes a replay of someone else's) berating us for a perceived flaw.

Sometimes it's so automatic, we may not notice there is a voice at all. Though its impact is present in our mind, body, or heart... feeling badly about who we are, what we've done, or what's (*im*)possible for our lives.

Take a few moments to reflect on the phrases you use to judge yourself. While there can be different ones depending on the situation, we often tend to have a few we use regularly, in a variety of situations.

The following are just a few examples of how it may sound...

I can't believe I did that. I'm such a(n)_______ !

I should know better than to _______ .

That's what I get for _______ !

Who am I kidding, I could never _______ .

I'll never be ______ .

What thoughts, feelings, or reactions came up as you read this?

What thoughts, ideas, or beliefs do you tend to repeat?

Is there anything that surprised you?

Take a moment to check in with your body. What do you notice?

Write an apology to your inner child for being so unkind to her/him.

Check in with your body again. What do you notice?

When complete,

Inhale ... Self-Forgiveness

Exhale... Self-Judgment

____

____

____

____

____

____

Courage is feeling the full range of all my emotions.

Feelings are not inherently good or bad. Whether they feel "positive" or "negative" in a particular moment, they are a lens to help us connect within and recognize if there is something we may need to tend to.

Expressing "positive" feelings often feels quite natural. We generally don't feel the need or desire to deny or minimize feeling happy, excited, content, peaceful, etc. We don't typically worry about what someone will think if we're feeling or expressing any of these types of feelings.

Expressing anger, disappointment, sadness, loneliness, hurt, or fear can feel much more challenging, for a variety of reasons.

Take a moment to reflect on the last time you felt sad, disappointed, hurt, angry, or any other perceived bad feeling.

Did you criticize, judge, or berate yourself? Tell yourself you shouldn't feel what you were feeling? Did you tell yourself you were being weak? Maybe that you needed to toughen up or pull yourself up by your bootstraps? Did you remind yourself there's so much to be grateful for so you shouldn't feel ________ ?

All of these statements reinforce long-held (false) beliefs about not being worthy exactly as you are, fully human with a range of emotions and experiences.

Allowing ourselves to feel the full range of human emotion takes courage. If we deny the "bad" feelings, we also diminish our capacity to fully feel the "good" feelings.

Consider the situation you identified above and write a note to her/him from a loving, accepting and supportive place.

If this feels challenging, consider what you would say to someone you care about who is criticizing themselves for feeling similarly.

When complete,

Inhale... Courage

Exhale... Shame

I am perfectly imperfect.

We tend to focus on the things we don't do.

We get caught up in the mistakes we've made... even the really small ones, or perceived failures.

We forget about the positive things we've done or the success we've achieved. Instead, focusing on the one thing that did not meet our (or someone else's) expectations, wasn't perfect, or wasn't completed.

Being happy, healthy, and free requires us to release the idea that we must be, look, or do things in a specific way.

It requires us to give ourselves the same grace we give others when we see, experience, or know their imperfection... either in a moment or maybe part of their quirkiness or struggle.

What imperfection (something you tend to hold onto that makes you believe you're unworthy, not enough, a failure, etc.) can you begin to practice accepting? If it's a quirk, maybe you can even begin to appreciate?!

When complete,

Inhale...Self-Acceptance

Exhale...Self-Ridicule

I am as deserving of my compassion, understanding, and kindness as those I love.

Take a moment and notice what came up as you read the affirmation, any thoughts or body sensations.

Was there an immediate rebuttal? Did you come up with all the reasons why it can't be true for you? Did you think if I really knew who you are or what you've done, I wouldn't believe this?

These types of rebuttals are how we reinforce our long-held (false) beliefs about who we are.

Take a deep breath and repeat the opening affirmation... I am as deserving of my compassion, understanding, and kindness as those I love.

Let yourself *be* with this truth as you move through a few rounds of breath.

Check in with yourself. What do you notice in your thoughts or body?

When complete,

Inhale... Self-Love

Exhale... Guilt

My mistakes do not define my worthiness.

I'd like you to think of something you view as a failure or mistake (the word you use might be different... screwed up, messed up, incapable, etc.). It could be something from today or a long time ago.

Notice how you feel when thinking about it. Notice what thoughts come to mind about it and yourself.

Does it bring more negative thoughts?

Does it bring up shame, guilt, or embarrassment?

Is it a reminder of why you're not enough, worthy, or deserving? Or maybe a reminder of why you're bad or wrong in some way?

However it leaves you feeling, I'd like you now to try to connect with either self-compassion or self-forgiveness (whichever feels most relevant).

We all make mistakes. Sometimes they're big. Sometimes they're small. Sometimes they impact someone else. Sometimes they impact only us.

None of us can excel at everything. We all fall short of meeting our or someone else's (often unrealistic) expectations.

NONE of this defines who we are. **NONE** of this makes us bad, unworthy, or unlovable.

We are all perfectly imperfect human beings. It's in this humanness we find connection.

Write a note of grace or forgiveness for yourself for this mistake or perceived failure.

When complete,

Inhale... Love

Exhale... Constriction

Reflect on your time in school (approx. 5-16 years old) and what types of thoughts or ideas you held about yourself... who you were, what you were (*in*)capable of, what you were "good" or "bad" at.

Whether it was academics, extracurricular activities, or our friend group (or lack of friend group) most of us developed a negative idea (belief) about ourselves through these experiences.

Maybe it's something you were very aware of at the time or it may be something you recognize upon reflection.

Write what some of those thoughts are and if there is a particular experience tied to your reflection, write that too.

Notice the path your mind has taken. Notice where and how this remembrance shows up in your body.

From a place of compassion, what would you like to say to that child who experienced some level of uncertainty, doubt, fear, judgment, or shame?

When complete,

Inhale... Acceptance

Exhale... Isolation

Put your right hand over your heart and put your left hand over your right.

Feel the warmth and energy of your hands penetrate into your heart space.

Take a few rounds of breath, feeling your heartbeat.

Send kindness and love as you imagine warm light moving through your hands, connecting with your heart and flowing into any spaces that feel tension or pain (emotional or physical).

Let yourself *be* here for a few moments or as long as you like. Take your time.

When you're ready, what did you notice coming up for you (thoughts, emotions, or reactions)?

When complete,

Inhale... Peace

Exhale... Uncertainty

"The reason we struggle with insecurity is because we compare our behind-the-scenes with everyone else's highlight reel. ~ Steve Furtick

Comparing ourselves to others is one of the most destructive things we can do to our sense of self. Yet, most of us do it quite naturally. Many of us do it quite frequently.

We become so adept at comparison, we can find something about almost anyone to compare ourselves to in a way that leaves us feeling *less than*.

We often don't even recognize that others may have a behind-the-scenes. We automatically assume their entire life is a highlight reel.

What we fail to recognize is that it is possible, even likely, that we hold traits, strengths, successes that others may be comparing themselves against.

What ways do you tend to compare yourself? Sometimes it's the same few things we compare over and over to a variety of people. Other times, there may be a particular person or a few people with whom we can always find something to compare. (These are often people we tend to feel envious of.)

You have a multitude of highlight reels. Take a few moments to reflect on some of your own. Make a list. Remind yourself there is much for you to feel good about.

Notice any thoughts or sensations in your body.

When complete,

Inhale... Pride

Exhale... Comparison

One of the most insidious ways we judge ourselves is by "shoulding". On a particularly challenging day, you may say some form of "*I should*" _________ or "*I shouldn't*" _________ up to 100+ times.

There's a good possibility you are unaware of how frequently these statements are present.

Yet, those two words can deeply affect how you feel about yourself.

Every time you repeat one of these statements, you are judging yourself. Each time you judge yourself you are reinforcing a long-held false belief. With each act of reinforcement, you move further away from self-acceptance.

We often use these words as a way to justify feelings of guilt or being undeserving.

Are there times that come to mind when you've done this? How did it leave you feeling? What belief did it reinforce?

How can you express kindness, understanding, or forgiveness to yourself for the things you judge yourself for?

Try to be mindful and practice not using these words, even just for a few days. You might be surprised how automatically you use them.

When complete,

Inhale… Self-acceptance

Exhale… Regret

And I said to my body, softly, "I want to be your friend". It took a long breath and replied, "I have been waiting my whole life for this".
– Nayyirah Waheed

Take a moment to read that again. Close your eyes and notice what is present in your thoughts or in your body.

So much of our self-criticism comes from ideas we hold about our bodies. Generally, ideas created by unrealistic standards or comparisons.

We judge, we neglect, and we abuse the incredible vessel which nourishes our heart, stores our memories, and fuels action on behalf of our desires.

We focus on the attribute that doesn't meet some arbitrary standard; a part that doesn't work in the way someone else's might; the muscles, organs, or limbs that have "let us down"; perceived flaws of our skin... color, freckles, moles, blemishes, sagging or aging; the size... too big, too small, too tall, too short, too much of this or too little of that.

I imagine you would never express, or even think, these judgments about someone you care about.

You wouldn't because you know these things do not define who they are. And, you have no expectation their body should or needs to be a particular way for you to value them.

Our bodies, even when they don't work or function optimally are quite

miraculous.
Your body knows when it needs to be refueled and sends you signals. It creates pain to let you know to back off the stress you're putting on it. It whispers, or if needed, yells when you're not following its intuitive knowing. If you are able-bodied, it automatically knows how to get you from point A to point B, generally with beautiful fluidity. It knows how to heal injuries and illnesses.

It feels... love, joy, sadness, grief, connection, compassion, and acceptance.

Take a moment to notice what is present for you.

Are you connected to your body? Has your mind wandered somewhere else? If so, it's okay. Just come back and reconnect.

How do you criticize or judge your body?

Take a few moments to connect with a sense of appreciation for all your body does. All the strength it possesses. All the illnesses it's fought. All the ways it allows you to move through your days and your life.

The way your heart knows how to beat, your lungs know how to breathe, your eyes know to blink, and your muscles know when you need a good tip to toe stretch.

Make a list of some of the things you appreciate about your body.

Write an apology to a part of your body you've mistreated, in thoughts or actions.

Become friends with your body… it's been waiting your whole life.

When complete,

Inhale… Gratitude

Exhale… Expectation

You can search throughout the entire universe for someone who is more deserving of your love and affection than you are yourself, and that person is not to be found anywhere. You yourself, as much as anybody in the entire universe deserve your love and affection.

- Buddha

What negative beliefs have you reinforced about yourself today or in the past couple of days (unworthy, not enough, failure, undeserving)?

What words did you use to judge yourself?

Take a moment to imagine a child in the same type of situation in which you said these harsh things to yourself.

Would you feel the same way about that child or speak (or yell) those words to her or him?

I can't know the answer for sure but, I suspect you would likely never speak to a child in the same way you speak to yourself, even if you were disappointed in the child's behavior.

What do you notice in your thoughts or body? Take a few moments to sit with this.

Write a note of compassion or kindness to yourself as you were in the moment in time you identified above.

When complete,

Inhale... Tenderness

Exhale... Fear

Reflect on a choice you've made that you find yourself going back to repeatedly as evidence of your "poor judgment".

It could be someone you did or didn't date or marry, a job you did or didn't take, the new town you did or didn't move to, not trusting yourself, or a mistake you've made. There are many more possibilities you may identify.

We all have at least a few experiences we return to as a way to reinforce a negative belief about who we are.

Ask yourself, is it really true that this experience proves you don't have the ability to make good choices?

Of course not!

There are certainly a number of things someone close to you could identify that, at least to them, shows you have good judgment.

Write a statement reframing what you say to yourself about this choice from a place of understanding.

It may even be possible that you learned something about yourself as a result of this choice.

When complete,

Inhale… Understanding

Exhale… Regret

I have not given up. And for that, I can be proud.

I know this statement is true for you because you are reading this.

There is so much within you to be proud of!

Yes, YOU!

We often have the belief that we can only be proud when we reach some idea of perfection. Which, of course, doesn't exist.

This can create a continual cycle of striving for the unattainable with an expectation that if we just work harder, become better or smarter we will have finally *earned* the right to feel proud, only to be disappointed with ourselves when it isn't perfect, or we don't feel how we hoped we would.

Write a letter to the little you, somewhere between the age of 5-12, expressing your pride in who she/he was or what she/he accomplished. Maybe it's something that, at the time, you saw as a failure or not being enough.

Before you start, notice what is present for you, in your thoughts and your body.

Check in with yourself after writing the letter, noticing what thoughts, feelings, or body sensations are present.

When complete,

Inhale... Pride

Exhale... Uncertainty

I am worthy and lovable with all my imperfections.

Reflect on yourself as a child between the ages of 13-17. Identify a time or experience when you felt "less than". Maybe you questioned or compared your academic or athletic ability. Maybe a friendship hit a rough spot or ended. Maybe some difficult things were going on at home.

Write a letter to this teenager expressing your pride in who they were or what they accomplished. It's okay if you can't seem to identify something right away. There are many things others could point to for you. Even if you don't feel it, try accepting one (or some) of those to write about.

Before you start, notice what is present for you, in your thoughts and your body.

Check in with yourself after writing the letter, noticing what thoughts, feelings, or body sensations are present.

When complete,

Inhale... Love

Exhale... Self-doubt

An area that can create lasting shame is judgment about how we've coped with challenging emotions and experiences.

Unfortunately, we are not directly taught as children how to cope when feelings or experiences are challenging. Therefore, it is our automatic survival mechanisms that kick in to help us best navigate whatever challenge is present.

This is true whether your childhood was incredibly traumatic or quite calm and enjoyable.

All children experience some level of difficulty. It's part of our natural development and human experience.

Because children do not yet have the brain development nor freedom to consider possible options and determine what might work best, we use what is available to us.

Over time, the coping mechanisms we developed as children become "hardwired" so that anytime we struggle these automatic responses kick in to help us get through it. Whether it's something fairly mild or traumatic.

In our teenage and adult lives, these coping mechanisms can develop into behaviors we feel ashamed of.

Addictive behaviors (drugs, alcohol, shopping, gambling, sex, disordered eating or exercise), self-harm, anger or projection, avoidance of uncomfortable feelings or situations, and self-sabotaging behaviors (procrastination, risky sexual encounters) are the most common.

While we may not have learned healthy ways of coping as children, we can do so now. *Resetting our automatic responses to difficulty is possible with practice, conscious effort and self-compassion as you learn new ways of responding.*

What are your "go-to" ways of coping? Have you felt shame, embarrassment, or guilt about the ways you've coped?

What have you believed your coping mechanisms say about who you are?

Most of us have or do cope in ways that are not helpful in our adult lives, possibly even damaging to us. Sometimes our ways of coping can impact others.

None of this defines who you are as a human being. None of it dictates your worthiness, lovability, or capability.

And, none of it is something to be ashamed of.

Take a moment to notice what is present in your body and your thoughts.

Take some time and write a note of forgiveness to yourself for anything you feel badly about doing or engaging in, acknowledging the truth of the challenges while also extending understanding and compassion.

When complete,

Inhale... Self-forgiveness

Exhale... Shame

Today you are you, that is truer than true. There is no one alive who is youer than you. - Dr. Seuss

In what ways have you believed you are "too much"?

Too much energy, too sensitive, too introverted, too extroverted, too angry, too accommodating, too independent, too loud, too happy, too sad, too self-contemplative, too rigid, too free-spirited.

This is not an exhaustive list but hopefully, it helps you recognize some of the ideas you may hold about yourself.

If you think you're too much of something you are judging yourself. You believe it is somehow wrong and you would be a better or more likable person if you were just not quite so ________ .

Something to consider, what if it's not too much? What if this characteristic or feeling is part of what makes you whole?

What if becoming less ________ meant other incredible parts of your personality were also diminished?

What if, you as you are, is exactly who your future best friend, partner, or boss has been waiting for?

What if, you as you are, is exactly who YOU've been longing to love and accept?

Notice what is present in your thoughts and body. If possible, look in a mirror and notice any expression on your face.

Write a note of full, complete, and wholehearted acceptance of who you are. You can write this to your child self and the person you are in this moment.

When complete,

Inhale... Satisfaction

Exhale... Comparison

I am always, in all ways, more than enough.

In what ways have you believed you are "not enough"?

Not good, smart, pretty, athletic, fit, kind, grateful, strong, successful, or simply, Just. Not. Enough.

There are so many ways we may believe we're not enough. There are no shortages of experiences that serve to reinforce the ways we believe this. Experiences we hold onto as evidence or proof.

The truth is, there is always room for improvement for each of us. But there is no perfection. This means, as humans there will always be parts of who we are, what we do, our capacities and capabilities that are more than enough in any given moment.

Take a moment to reflect on all the ways you are and have been enough. From the seemingly small to the "Wow! I can't believe I did that."

If you're having trouble identifying something right away, it's okay. It's not that it doesn't exist, it's just that it's been hidden away. All of these practices are designed to help bring these truths to your conscious awareness, leaving less room for negative and false beliefs.

Write a note of appreciation for who you are now. Not the person you believe will be worthy when you achieve whatever arbitrary marker you've designated as enough.

Maybe another day come back and write a note to your child self who believed they were not enough.

When complete,

Inhale... Confidence

Exhale...Comparison

The most terrifying thing is to accept oneself completely.
- Carl Jung

Take a moment to reflect on this quote. Notice any thoughts, feelings, or sensations in your body.

It may seem counterintuitive, but it truly can be terrifying to consider the possibility of completely changing who you believe you are and how you move through the world, even when it's a positive change.

You've likely held onto ideas about who you are for years, possibly decades. Though the ideas may not feel good and may lead to struggle, you are familiar with the patterns and feelings. You've learned how to navigate your days, the ups and downs.

Who are you if you're not the person you've believed is deserving of all your judgment, criticism, and shame?

Accepting yourself, as you are, in every moment is the necessary foundation for becoming happy, healthy, whole, and free.

Accepting yourself wholly doesn't mean you think you're perfect. It means you recognize that perfection is not required to be worthy. To be valued and loved.

It means you can be valued and loved, not *despite* your mistakes or imperfections, but *because* of them.

Because, mistakes and imperfections make you human, and when one human can see another human as they are, knowing we are all imperfect, there is an acceptance and connection between them.

What things might you open yourself up to if you believed you were worthy, deserving, or capable of having or achieving it?

Take a moment to close your eyes (if it feels comfortable to do so) and visualize what a day in your life might look like. Imagine the difference you would feel in your body if you were able to feel the freedom of deeply rooted self-acceptance and the impact that might have on how you move throughout your day.

You are deserving of that!

When complete,

Inhale... Freedom

Exhale... Limitations

____

____

____

____

____

Take a few moments to consider the myriad ways you've judged, criticized, blamed, berated, and shamed yourself at different points in your life.

Take a breath and remind yourself you are not the person you've tried to make yourself believe you are each time you've done this.

You are worthy, deserving, and always, in *all ways,* more than enough in each and every moment.

You are the light that makes the stars shine.

Write a letter to yourself, the you who's navigated life's challenges, made mistakes, loved fiercely, and hurt immensely apologizing for being so incredibly hard on this perfectly imperfect human. Let her/him know you are committed to being mindful of showing the same kindness and understanding to them you show to those you love.

When complete,

Inhale... Love

Exhale... Self-doubt

Inhale... Tenderness

Exhale...Fear

Inhale... Kindness

Exhale... Criticism

Inhale... Acceptance

Exhale... Judgment

Inhale ... Confidence

Exhale... Comparison

Inhale... Joy

Exhale... Constriction

Take a moment to honor all you've done through this journal.

You've created space to take care of yourself. You've allowed yourself to *be with* experiences and feelings you may have worked hard at denying or pushing away. You've opened your heart to seeing yourself through a more accepting and compassionate lens. You've done the courageous work of connecting within so you may heal all that's held you back from honoring your whole self.

Remember, cultivating self-compassion and self-acceptance is a *process* and a *practice*. Please don't think you should have mastered self-compassion or never experience self-doubt again.

You will need to continue to be mindful and intentional about replacing the automatic (negative) thoughts with truth (compassion).

Coming back to these prompts and practices will help you do that.

Each time you return, your mind will be in a bit of a different place than it was the previous time(s). This will allow you to work through the myriad places your mind can take you in a given moment.

With continued practice you may be able to go a bit deeper. Over time, you'll notice it's a bit easier... more natural, to connect with kindness, understanding, and compassion.

I've included additional journaling pages at the end for you to continue your process.

Remember, we are all

perfectly imperfect

AND

still worthy of our

desires, happiness,

connection and love.

Peggy Oliveira, MSW is a trauma therapist, social worker, and mentor. She's known as the Survivor Whisperer® for her soulful way of helping clients and followers understand the connections between their current (and possibly life-long) struggles and core wounding, creating an opening for deep healing.

Peggy is the founder of Courageous Journeys®, an online space for learning, healing, and connecting via 1:1 mentoring, courses and groups, and a YouTube channel where she shares information on healing emotional wounding. She also facilitates in-person individual and group healing retreats.

You can learn more and connect with Peggy in the following ways:

www.courageousjourneys.com
www.facebook.com/courageousjourneys
www.youtube.com/peggyoliveiramsw